This Book Belongs To

Name: _____

Address: _____

_____

Email: _____

Phone: _____

Diamond Painting Photo

Additional notes: _____

_____

_____

_____

_____

_____

_____

_____

_____

_____

_____

Design/kit name: _____

If custom, describe: _____

Dimensions: _____

Drill type: Square ▽   Round ▽   Special ▽

Drill total: _____   Coverage: Full ▽   Partial ▽

Number of different drill colors: _____

Website purchased from: _____

Seller/store name: _____

Price: _____   On Sale: Yes ▽   No ▽

Shipping cost: _____   Estimated arrival date: _____

Date purchased: _____

Date arrived: _____

Quality of product: _____

Any missing items: _____

Customer service notes: _____

_____

If the kit was a gift, who was it from? _____

Date gift received: _____   Occasion: _____

Date started: _____   Date completed: _____

Estimated total hours to complete: _____

Difficulty level: Beginner ▽   Intermediate ▽   Advanced ▽

What I did with the finished piece:

Kept it ▽   Gifted it ▽   Sold it ▽   Other _____

If gifted or sold, person received: _____

If sold, what was the price? _____

Framed: Yes ▽   No ▽

My overall rating of this project: ▽ ▽ ▽ ▽ ▽

Diamond Painting Photo

Additional notes: _____

_____

_____

_____

_____

_____

_____

_____

_____

_____

_____

Design/kit name: _____

If custom, describe: _____

Dimensions: _____

Drill type: Square ▽   Round ▽   Special ▽

Drill total: _____   Coverage: Full ▽   Partial ▽

Number of different drill colors: _____

Website purchased from: _____

Seller/store name: _____

Price: _____   On Sale: Yes ▽   No ▽

Shipping cost: _____   Estimated arrival date: _____

Date purchased: _____

Date arrived: _____

Quality of product: _____

Any missing items: _____

Customer service notes: _____

_____

If the kit was a gift, who was it from? _____

Date gift received: _____   Occasion: _____

Date started: _____   Date completed: _____

Estimated total hours to complete: _____

Difficulty level: Beginner ▽   Intermediate ▽   Advanced ▽

What I did with the finished piece:

Kept it ▽   Gifted it ▽   Sold it ▽   Other _____

If gifted or sold, person received: _____

If sold, what was the price? _____

Framed: Yes ▽   No ▽

My overall rating of this project: ▽ ▽ ▽ ▽ ▽

Diamond Painting Photo

Additional notes: _____

_____

_____

_____

_____

_____

_____

_____

_____

_____

_____

Design/kit name: _____

If custom, describe: _____

Dimensions: _____

Drill type: Square ▽   Round ▽   Special ▽

Drill total: _____   Coverage: Full ▽   Partial ▽

Number of different drill colors: _____

Website purchased from: _____

Seller/store name: _____

Price: _____   On Sale: Yes ▽   No ▽

Shipping cost: _____   Estimated arrival date: _____

Date purchased: _____

Date arrived: _____

Quality of product: _____

Any missing items: _____

Customer service notes: _____

_____

If the kit was a gift, who was it from? _____

Date gift received: _____   Occasion: _____

Date started: _____   Date completed: _____

Estimated total hours to complete: _____

Difficulty level: Beginner ▽   Intermediate ▽   Advanced ▽

What I did with the finished piece:

Kept it ▽   Gifted it ▽   Sold it ▽   Other _____

If gifted or sold, person received: _____

If sold, what was the price? _____

Framed: Yes ▽   No ▽

My overall rating of this project: ▽ ▽ ▽ ▽ ▽

Diamond Painting Photo

Additional notes: _____

_____
_____
_____
_____
_____
_____
_____
_____
_____
_____
_____

Design/kit name: _____

If custom, describe: _____

Dimensions: _____

Drill type: Square ▽   Round ▽   Special ▽

Drill total: _____   Coverage: Full ▽   Partial ▽

Number of different drill colors: _____

Website purchased from: _____

Seller/store name: _____

Price: _____   On Sale: Yes ▽   No ▽

Shipping cost: _____   Estimated arrival date: _____

Date purchased: _____

Date arrived: _____

Quality of product: _____

Any missing items: _____

Customer service notes: _____

_____

If the kit was a gift, who was it from? _____

Date gift received: _____   Occasion: _____

Date started: _____   Date completed: _____

Estimated total hours to complete: _____

Difficulty level: Beginner ▽   Intermediate ▽   Advanced ▽

What I did with the finished piece:

Kept it ▽   Gifted it ▽   Sold it ▽   Other _____

If gifted or sold, person received: _____

If sold, what was the price? _____

Framed: Yes ▽   No ▽

My overall rating of this project: ▽ ▽ ▽ ▽ ▽

Diamond Painting Photo

Additional notes: _____

_____
_____
_____
_____
_____
_____
_____
_____
_____
_____
_____

Design/kit name: _____

If custom, describe: _____

Dimensions: _____

Drill type: Square ▽   Round ▽   Special ▽

Drill total: _____   Coverage: Full ▽   Partial ▽

Number of different drill colors: _____

Website purchased from: _____

Seller/store name: _____

Price: _____   On Sale: Yes ▽   No ▽

Shipping cost: _____   Estimated arrival date: _____

Date purchased: _____

Date arrived: _____

Quality of product: _____

Any missing items: _____

Customer service notes: _____

_____

If the kit was a gift, who was it from? _____

Date gift received: _____   Occasion: _____

Date started: _____   Date completed: _____

Estimated total hours to complete: _____

Difficulty level: Beginner ▽   Intermediate ▽   Advanced ▽

What I did with the finished piece:

Kept it ▽   Gifted it ▽   Sold it ▽   Other _____

If gifted or sold, person received: _____

If sold, what was the price? _____

Framed: Yes ▽   No ▽

My overall rating of this project: ▽ ▽ ▽ ▽ ▽

Diamond Painting Photo

Additional notes: _____

_____
_____
_____
_____
_____
_____
_____
_____
_____
_____
_____

Design/kit name: _____

If custom, describe: _____

Dimensions: _____

Drill type:　　Square ▽　　　Round ▽　　　Special ▽

Drill total: _____　　　Coverage:　Full ▽　Partial ▽

Number of different drill colors: _____

Website purchased from: _____

Seller/store name: _____

Price: _____　　On Sale:　Yes ▽　　No ▽

Shipping cost: _____　Estimated arrival date: _____

Date purchased: _____

Date arrived: _____

Quality of product: _____

Any missing items: _____

Customer service notes: _____

_____

If the kit was a gift, who was it from? _____

Date gift received: _____　Occasion: _____

Date started: _____　Date completed: _____

Estimated total hours to complete: _____

Difficulty level:　Beginner ▽　　Intermediate ▽　　Advanced ▽

What I did with the finished piece:

Kept it ▽　　Gifted it ▽　　Sold it ▽　　Other _____

If gifted or sold, person received: _____

If sold, what was the price? _____

Framed:　Yes ▽　　No ▽

My overall rating of this project:　　▽ ▽ ▽ ▽ ▽

Diamond Painting Photo

Additional notes: _____

_____
_____
_____
_____
_____
_____
_____
_____
_____
_____
_____

Design/kit name: _____

If custom, describe: _____

Dimensions: _____

Drill type: Square   Round   Special

Drill total: _____   Coverage: Full   Partial

Number of different drill colors: _____

Website purchased from: _____

Seller/store name: _____

Price: _____   On Sale: Yes   No

Shipping cost: _____   Estimated arrival date: _____

Date purchased: _____

Date arrived: _____

Quality of product: _____

Any missing items: _____

Customer service notes: _____

_____

If the kit was a gift, who was it from? _____

Date gift received: _____   Occasion: _____

Date started: _____   Date completed: _____

Estimated total hours to complete: _____

Difficulty level: Beginner   Intermediate   Advanced

What I did with the finished piece:

Kept it   Gifted it   Sold it   Other _____

If gifted or sold, person received: _____

If sold, what was the price? _____

Framed: Yes   No

My overall rating of this project:

Diamond Painting Photo

Additional notes: _____

_____
_____
_____
_____
_____
_____
_____
_____
_____
_____

Design/kit name: _____

If custom, describe: _____

Dimensions: _____

Drill type: Square ▽   Round ▽   Special ▽

Drill total: _____   Coverage: Full ▽   Partial ▽

Number of different drill colors: _____

Website purchased from: _____

Seller/store name: _____

Price: _____   On Sale: Yes ▽   No ▽

Shipping cost: _____   Estimated arrival date: _____

Date purchased: _____

Date arrived: _____

Quality of product: _____

Any missing items: _____

Customer service notes: _____

_____

If the kit was a gift, who was it from? _____

Date gift received: _____   Occasion: _____

Date started: _____   Date completed: _____

Estimated total hours to complete: _____

Difficulty level: Beginner ▽   Intermediate ▽   Advanced ▽

What I did with the finished piece:

Kept it ▽   Gifted it ▽   Sold it ▽   Other _____

If gifted or sold, person received: _____

If sold, what was the price? _____

Framed: Yes ▽   No ▽

My overall rating of this project: ▽ ▽ ▽ ▽ ▽

Diamond Painting Photo

Additional notes: _____

_____
_____
_____
_____
_____
_____
_____
_____
_____
_____

Design/kit name: _____

If custom, describe: _____

Dimensions: _____

Drill type: Square ▽   Round ▽   Special ▽

Drill total: _____   Coverage: Full ▽   Partial ▽

Number of different drill colors: _____

Website purchased from: _____

Seller/store name: _____

Price: _____   On Sale: Yes ▽   No ▽

Shipping cost: _____   Estimated arrival date: _____

Date purchased: _____

Date arrived: _____

Quality of product: _____

Any missing items: _____

Customer service notes: _____

_____

If the kit was a gift, who was it from? _____

Date gift received: _____   Occasion: _____

Date started: _____   Date completed: _____

Estimated total hours to complete: _____

Difficulty level: Beginner ▽   Intermediate ▽   Advanced ▽

What I did with the finished piece:

Kept it ▽   Gifted it ▽   Sold it ▽   Other _____

If gifted or sold, person received: _____

If sold, what was the price? _____

Framed: Yes ▽   No ▽

My overall rating of this project: ▽ ▽ ▽ ▽ ▽

Diamond Painting Photo

Additional notes: _____

_____
_____
_____
_____
_____
_____
_____
_____
_____
_____
_____

Design/kit name: _____

If custom, describe: _____

Dimensions: _____

Drill type: Square ▽   Round ▽   Special ▽

Drill total: _____   Coverage: Full ▽   Partial ▽

Number of different drill colors: _____

Website purchased from: _____

Seller/store name: _____

Price: _____   On Sale: Yes ▽   No ▽

Shipping cost: _____   Estimated arrival date: _____

Date purchased: _____

Date arrived: _____

Quality of product: _____

Any missing items: _____

Customer service notes: _____

_____

If the kit was a gift, who was it from? _____

Date gift received: _____   Occasion: _____

Date started: _____   Date completed: _____

Estimated total hours to complete: _____

Difficulty level: Beginner ▽   Intermediate ▽   Advanced ▽

What I did with the finished piece:

Kept it ▽   Gifted it ▽   Sold it ▽   Other _____

If gifted or sold, person received: _____

If sold, what was the price? _____

Framed: Yes ▽   No ▽

My overall rating of this project: ▽ ▽ ▽ ▽ ▽

Diamond Painting Photo

Additional notes: _____

_____

_____

_____

_____

_____

_____

_____

_____

_____

Design/kit name: _____

If custom, describe: _____

Dimensions: _____

Drill type:　Square ▽　　Round ▽　　Special ▽

Drill total: _____　Coverage:　Full ▽　Partial ▽

Number of different drill colors: _____

Website purchased from: _____

Seller/store name: _____

Price: _____　On Sale:　Yes ▽　　No ▽

Shipping cost: _____　Estimated arrival date: _____

Date purchased: _____

Date arrived: _____

Quality of product: _____

Any missing items: _____

Customer service notes: _____

_____

If the kit was a gift, who was it from? _____

Date gift received: _____　Occasion: _____

Date started: _____　Date completed: _____

Estimated total hours to complete: _____

Difficulty level:　Beginner ▽　Intermediate ▽　Advanced ▽

What I did with the finished piece:

Kept it ▽　　Gifted it ▽　　Sold it ▽　　Other _____

If gifted or sold, person received: _____

If sold, what was the price? _____

Framed:　Yes ▽　　No ▽

My overall rating of this project:　▽ ▽ ▽ ▽ ▽

Diamond Painting Photo

Additional notes: _____

_____
_____
_____
_____
_____
_____
_____
_____
_____
_____

Design/kit name: _____

If custom, describe: _____

Dimensions: _____

Drill type: Square ▽   Round ▽   Special ▽

Drill total: _____   Coverage: Full ▽   Partial ▽

Number of different drill colors: _____

Website purchased from: _____

Seller/store name: _____

Price: _____   On Sale: Yes ▽   No ▽

Shipping cost: _____   Estimated arrival date: _____

Date purchased: _____

Date arrived: _____

Quality of product: _____

Any missing items: _____

Customer service notes: _____

_____

If the kit was a gift, who was it from? _____

Date gift received: _____   Occasion: _____

Date started: _____   Date completed: _____

Estimated total hours to complete: _____

Difficulty level: Beginner ▽   Intermediate ▽   Advanced ▽

What I did with the finished piece:

Kept it ▽   Gifted it ▽   Sold it ▽   Other _____

If gifted or sold, person received: _____

If sold, what was the price? _____

Framed: Yes ▽   No ▽

My overall rating of this project: ▽ ▽ ▽ ▽ ▽

Diamond Painting Photo

Additional notes: _____

_____

_____

_____

_____

_____

_____

_____

_____

_____

_____

Design/kit name: _____

If custom, describe: _____

Dimensions: _____

Drill type: Square ▽   Round ▽   Special ▽

Drill total: _____   Coverage: Full ▽   Partial ▽

Number of different drill colors: _____

Website purchased from: _____

Seller/store name: _____

Price: _____   On Sale: Yes ▽   No ▽

Shipping cost: _____   Estimated arrival date: _____

Date purchased: _____

Date arrived: _____

Quality of product: _____

Any missing items: _____

Customer service notes: _____

_____

If the kit was a gift, who was it from? _____

Date gift received: _____   Occasion: _____

Date started: _____   Date completed: _____

Estimated total hours to complete: _____

Difficulty level: Beginner ▽   Intermediate ▽   Advanced ▽

What I did with the finished piece:

Kept it ▽   Gifted it ▽   Sold it ▽   Other _____

If gifted or sold, person received: _____

If sold, what was the price? _____

Framed: Yes ▽   No ▽

My overall rating of this project: ▽ ▽ ▽ ▽ ▽

Diamond Painting Photo

Additional notes: _____

_____
_____
_____
_____
_____
_____
_____
_____
_____
_____

Design/kit name: _____

If custom, describe: _____

Dimensions: _____

Drill type: Square ▽   Round ▽   Special ▽

Drill total: _____   Coverage: Full ▽   Partial ▽

Number of different drill colors: _____

Website purchased from: _____

Seller/store name: _____

Price: _____   On Sale: Yes ▽   No ▽

Shipping cost: _____   Estimated arrival date: _____

Date purchased: _____

Date arrived: _____

Quality of product: _____

Any missing items: _____

Customer service notes: _____

_____

If the kit was a gift, who was it from? _____

Date gift received: _____   Occasion: _____

Date started: _____   Date completed: _____

Estimated total hours to complete: _____

Difficulty level: Beginner ▽   Intermediate ▽   Advanced ▽

What I did with the finished piece:

Kept it ▽   Gifted it ▽   Sold it ▽   Other _____

If gifted or sold, person received: _____

If sold, what was the price? _____

Framed: Yes ▽   No ▽

My overall rating of this project: ▽ ▽ ▽ ▽ ▽

Diamond Painting Photo

Additional notes: _____

_____

_____

_____

_____

_____

_____

_____

_____

_____

_____

Design/kit name: _____

If custom, describe: _____

Dimensions: _____

Drill type: Square ▽   Round ▽   Special ▽

Drill total: _____   Coverage: Full ▽   Partial ▽

Number of different drill colors: _____

Website purchased from: _____

Seller/store name: _____

Price: _____   On Sale: Yes ▽   No ▽

Shipping cost: _____   Estimated arrival date: _____

Date purchased: _____

Date arrived: _____

Quality of product: _____

Any missing items: _____

Customer service notes: _____

_____

If the kit was a gift, who was it from? _____

Date gift received: _____   Occasion: _____

Date started: _____   Date completed: _____

Estimated total hours to complete: _____

Difficulty level: Beginner ▽   Intermediate ▽   Advanced ▽

What I did with the finished piece:

Kept it ▽   Gifted it ▽   Sold it ▽   Other _____

If gifted or sold, person received: _____

If sold, what was the price? _____

Framed: Yes ▽   No ▽

My overall rating of this project: ▽ ▽ ▽ ▽ ▽

Diamond Painting Photo

Additional notes: _____

_____

_____

_____

_____

_____

_____

_____

_____

_____

_____

Design/kit name: _____

If custom, describe: _____

Dimensions: _____

Drill type: Square   Round   Special

Drill total: _____   Coverage: Full   Partial

Number of different drill colors: _____

Website purchased from: _____

Seller/store name: _____

Price: _____   On Sale: Yes   No

Shipping cost: _____   Estimated arrival date: _____

Date purchased: _____

Date arrived: _____

Quality of product: _____

Any missing items: _____

Customer service notes: _____

_____

If the kit was a gift, who was it from? _____

Date gift received: _____   Occasion: _____

Date started: _____   Date completed: _____

Estimated total hours to complete: _____

Difficulty level: Beginner   Intermediate   Advanced

What I did with the finished piece:

Kept it   Gifted it   Sold it   Other _____

If gifted or sold, person received: _____

If sold, what was the price? _____

Framed: Yes   No

My overall rating of this project:

Diamond Painting Photo

Additional notes: _____

_____

_____

_____

_____

_____

_____

_____

_____

_____

_____

Design/kit name: _____

If custom, describe: _____

Dimensions: _____

Drill type: Square $\triangledown$ Round $\triangledown$ Special $\triangledown$

Drill total: _____   Coverage: Full $\triangledown$ Partial $\triangledown$

Number of different drill colors: _____

Website purchased from: _____

Seller/store name: _____

Price: _____   On Sale: Yes $\triangledown$ No $\triangledown$

Shipping cost: _____   Estimated arrival date: _____

Date purchased: _____

Date arrived: _____

Quality of product: _____

Any missing items: _____

Customer service notes: _____

_____

If the kit was a gift, who was it from? _____

Date gift received: _____   Occasion: _____

Date started: _____   Date completed: _____

Estimated total hours to complete: _____

Difficulty level: Beginner $\triangledown$ Intermediate $\triangledown$ Advanced $\triangledown$

What I did with the finished piece:

Kept it $\triangledown$ Gifted it $\triangledown$ Sold it $\triangledown$ Other _____

If gifted or sold, person received: _____

If sold, what was the price? _____

Framed: Yes $\triangledown$ No $\triangledown$

My overall rating of this project: $\triangledown$ $\triangledown$ $\triangledown$ $\triangledown$ $\triangledown$

Diamond Painting Photo

Additional notes: _____

_____

_____

_____

_____

_____

_____

_____

_____

_____

_____

_____

Design/kit name: _____

If custom, describe: _____

Dimensions: _____

Drill type: Square ▽   Round ▽   Special ▽

Drill total: _____   Coverage: Full ▽   Partial ▽

Number of different drill colors: _____

Website purchased from: _____

Seller/store name: _____

Price: _____   On Sale: Yes ▽   No ▽

Shipping cost: _____   Estimated arrival date: _____

Date purchased: _____

Date arrived: _____

Quality of product: _____

Any missing items: _____

Customer service notes: _____

_____

If the kit was a gift, who was it from? _____

Date gift received: _____   Occasion: _____

Date started: _____   Date completed: _____

Estimated total hours to complete: _____

Difficulty level: Beginner ▽   Intermediate ▽   Advanced ▽

What I did with the finished piece:

Kept it ▽   Gifted it ▽   Sold it ▽   Other _____

If gifted or sold, person received: _____

If sold, what was the price? _____

Framed: Yes ▽   No ▽

My overall rating of this project: ▽ ▽ ▽ ▽ ▽

Diamond Painting Photo

Additional notes: _____

_____

_____

_____

_____

_____

_____

_____

_____

_____

_____

Design/kit name: _____

If custom, describe: _____

Dimensions: _____

Drill type:　　Square ▽　　　Round ▽　　　Special ▽

Drill total: _____　　Coverage:　Full ▽　Partial ▽

Number of different drill colors: _____

Website purchased from: _____

Seller/store name: _____

Price: _____　　On Sale:　Yes ▽　　No ▽

Shipping cost: _____　Estimated arrival date: _____

Date purchased: _____

Date arrived: _____

Quality of product: _____

Any missing items: _____

Customer service notes: _____

_____

If the kit was a gift, who was it from? _____

Date gift received: _____　Occasion: _____

Date started: _____　Date completed: _____

Estimated total hours to complete: _____

Difficulty level:　Beginner ▽　　Intermediate ▽　　Advanced ▽

What I did with the finished piece:

Kept it ▽　　Gifted it ▽　　Sold it ▽　　Other _____

If gifted or sold, person received: _____

If sold, what was the price? _____

Framed:　Yes ▽　　No ▽

My overall rating of this project:　▽ ▽ ▽ ▽ ▽

Diamond Painting Photo

Additional notes: _____

_____

_____

_____

_____

_____

_____

_____

_____

_____

_____

Design/kit name: _____

If custom, describe: _____

Dimensions: _____

Drill type: Square ▽   Round ▽   Special ▽

Drill total: _____   Coverage: Full ▽   Partial ▽

Number of different drill colors: _____

Website purchased from: _____

Seller/store name: _____

Price: _____   On Sale: Yes ▽   No ▽

Shipping cost: _____   Estimated arrival date: _____

Date purchased: _____

Date arrived: _____

Quality of product: _____

Any missing items: _____

Customer service notes: _____

_____

If the kit was a gift, who was it from? _____

Date gift received: _____   Occasion: _____

Date started: _____   Date completed: _____

Estimated total hours to complete: _____

Difficulty level: Beginner ▽   Intermediate ▽   Advanced ▽

What I did with the finished piece:

Kept it ▽   Gifted it ▽   Sold it ▽   Other _____

If gifted or sold, person received: _____

If sold, what was the price? _____

Framed: Yes ▽   No ▽

My overall rating of this project: ▽ ▽ ▽ ▽ ▽

Diamond Painting Photo

Additional notes: _____

_____

_____

_____

_____

_____

_____

_____

_____

_____

_____

_____

Design/kit name: _____

If custom, describe: _____

Dimensions: _____

Drill type:　Square　▽　　Round　▽　　Special　▽

Drill total: _____　Coverage:　Full　▽　Partial　▽

Number of different drill colors: _____

Website purchased from: _____

Seller/store name: _____

Price: _____　On Sale:　Yes　▽　　No　▽

Shipping cost: _____　Estimated arrival date: _____

Date purchased: _____

Date arrived: _____

Quality of product: _____

Any missing items: _____

Customer service notes: _____

_____

If the kit was a gift, who was it from? _____

Date gift received: _____　Occasion: _____

Date started: _____　Date completed: _____

Estimated total hours to complete: _____

Difficulty level:　Beginner　▽　　Intermediate　▽　　Advanced　▽

What I did with the finished piece:

Kept it　▽　　Gifted it　▽　　Sold it　▽　　Other _____

If gifted or sold, person received: _____

If sold, what was the price? _____

Framed:　Yes　▽　　No　▽

My overall rating of this project:　▽　▽　▽　▽　▽

```
┌─────────────────────────────────────────────┐
│                                               │
│                                               │
│                                               │
│                                               │
│                                               │
│             *Diamond Painting Photo*          │
│                                               │
│                                               │
│                                               │
│                                               │
│                                               │
│                                               │
└─────────────────────────────────────────────┘
```

Additional notes: _____

_____

_____

_____

_____

_____

_____

_____

_____

_____

_____

Design/kit name: _____

If custom, describe: _____

Dimensions: _____

Drill type: Square ▽   Round ▽   Special ▽

Drill total: _____   Coverage: Full ▽   Partial ▽

Number of different drill colors: _____

Website purchased from: _____

Seller/store name: _____

Price: _____   On Sale: Yes ▽   No ▽

Shipping cost: _____   Estimated arrival date: _____

Date purchased: _____

Date arrived: _____

Quality of product: _____

Any missing items: _____

Customer service notes: _____

_____

If the kit was a gift, who was it from? _____

Date gift received: _____   Occasion: _____

Date started: _____   Date completed: _____

Estimated total hours to complete: _____

Difficulty level: Beginner ▽   Intermediate ▽   Advanced ▽

What I did with the finished piece:

Kept it ▽   Gifted it ▽   Sold it ▽   Other _____

If gifted or sold, person received: _____

If sold, what was the price? _____

Framed: Yes ▽   No ▽

My overall rating of this project: ▽ ▽ ▽ ▽ ▽

Diamond Painting Photo

Additional notes: _____

_____

_____

_____

_____

_____

_____

_____

_____

_____

Design/kit name: _____

If custom, describe: _____

Dimensions: _____

Drill type: Square ▽   Round ▽   Special ▽

Drill total: _____   Coverage: Full ▽   Partial ▽

Number of different drill colors: _____

Website purchased from: _____

Seller/store name: _____

Price: _____   On Sale: Yes ▽   No ▽

Shipping cost: _____   Estimated arrival date: _____

Date purchased: _____

Date arrived: _____

Quality of product: _____

Any missing items: _____

Customer service notes: _____

_____

If the kit was a gift, who was it from? _____

Date gift received: _____   Occasion: _____

Date started: _____   Date completed: _____

Estimated total hours to complete: _____

Difficulty level: Beginner ▽   Intermediate ▽   Advanced ▽

What I did with the finished piece:

Kept it ▽   Gifted it ▽   Sold it ▽   Other _____

If gifted or sold, person received: _____

If sold, what was the price? _____

Framed: Yes ▽   No ▽

My overall rating of this project: ▽ ▽ ▽ ▽ ▽

Diamond Painting Photo

Additional notes: _____

_____

_____

_____

_____

_____

_____

_____

_____

_____

_____

Design/kit name: _____

If custom, describe: _____

Dimensions: _____

Drill type: Square ▽   Round ▽   Special ▽

Drill total: _____   Coverage: Full ▽   Partial ▽

Number of different drill colors: _____

Website purchased from: _____

Seller/store name: _____

Price: _____   On Sale: Yes ▽   No ▽

Shipping cost: _____   Estimated arrival date: _____

Date purchased: _____

Date arrived: _____

Quality of product: _____

Any missing items: _____

Customer service notes: _____

_____

If the kit was a gift, who was it from? _____

Date gift received: _____   Occasion: _____

Date started: _____   Date completed: _____

Estimated total hours to complete: _____

Difficulty level: Beginner ▽   Intermediate ▽   Advanced ▽

What I did with the finished piece:

Kept it ▽   Gifted it ▽   Sold it ▽   Other _____

If gifted or sold, person received: _____

If sold, what was the price? _____

Framed: Yes ▽   No ▽

My overall rating of this project: ▽ ▽ ▽ ▽ ▽

Diamond Painting Photo

Additional notes: _____

_____

_____

_____

_____

_____

_____

_____

_____

_____

_____

Design/kit name: _____

If custom, describe: _____

Dimensions: _____

Drill type: Square ▽   Round ▽   Special ▽

Drill total: _____   Coverage: Full ▽   Partial ▽

Number of different drill colors: _____

Website purchased from: _____

Seller/store name: _____

Price: _____   On Sale: Yes ▽   No ▽

Shipping cost: _____   Estimated arrival date: _____

Date purchased: _____

Date arrived: _____

Quality of product: _____

Any missing items: _____

Customer service notes: _____

_____

If the kit was a gift, who was it from? _____

Date gift received: _____   Occasion: _____

Date started: _____   Date completed: _____

Estimated total hours to complete: _____

Difficulty level: Beginner ▽   Intermediate ▽   Advanced ▽

What I did with the finished piece:

Kept it ▽   Gifted it ▽   Sold it ▽   Other _____

If gifted or sold, person received: _____

If sold, what was the price? _____

Framed: Yes ▽   No ▽

My overall rating of this project: ▽ ▽ ▽ ▽ ▽

Diamond Painting Photo

Additional notes: _____

_____

_____

_____

_____

_____

_____

_____

_____

_____

_____

Design/kit name: _____

If custom, describe: _____

Dimensions: _____

Drill type: Square ▽   Round ▽   Special ▽

Drill total: _____   Coverage: Full ▽   Partial ▽

Number of different drill colors: _____

Website purchased from: _____

Seller/store name: _____

Price: _____   On Sale: Yes ▽   No ▽

Shipping cost: _____   Estimated arrival date: _____

Date purchased: _____

Date arrived: _____

Quality of product: _____

Any missing items: _____

Customer service notes: _____

_____

If the kit was a gift, who was it from? _____

Date gift received: _____   Occasion: _____

Date started: _____   Date completed: _____

Estimated total hours to complete: _____

Difficulty level: Beginner ▽   Intermediate ▽   Advanced ▽

What I did with the finished piece:

Kept it ▽   Gifted it ▽   Sold it ▽   Other _____

If gifted or sold, person received: _____

If sold, what was the price? _____

Framed: Yes ▽   No ▽

My overall rating of this project: ▽ ▽ ▽ ▽ ▽

Diamond Painting Photo

Additional notes: _____

_____

_____

_____

_____

_____

_____

_____

_____

_____

Design/kit name: _____

If custom, describe: _____

Dimensions: _____

Drill type: Square ▽   Round ▽   Special ▽

Drill total: _____   Coverage: Full ▽   Partial ▽

Number of different drill colors: _____

Website purchased from: _____

Seller/store name: _____

Price: _____   On Sale: Yes ▽   No ▽

Shipping cost: _____   Estimated arrival date: _____

Date purchased: _____

Date arrived: _____

Quality of product: _____

Any missing items: _____

Customer service notes: _____

_____

If the kit was a gift, who was it from? _____

Date gift received: _____   Occasion: _____

Date started: _____   Date completed: _____

Estimated total hours to complete: _____

Difficulty level: Beginner ▽   Intermediate ▽   Advanced ▽

What I did with the finished piece:

Kept it ▽   Gifted it ▽   Sold it ▽   Other _____

If gifted or sold, person received: _____

If sold, what was the price? _____

Framed: Yes ▽   No ▽

My overall rating of this project: ▽ ▽ ▽ ▽ ▽

Diamond Painting Photo

Additional notes: _____

_____

_____

_____

_____

_____

_____

_____

_____

_____

_____

Design/kit name: _____

If custom, describe: _____

Dimensions: _____

Drill type: Square ▽   Round ▽   Special ▽

Drill total: _____   Coverage: Full ▽   Partial ▽

Number of different drill colors: _____

Website purchased from: _____

Seller/store name: _____

Price: _____   On Sale: Yes ▽   No ▽

Shipping cost: _____   Estimated arrival date: _____

Date purchased: _____

Date arrived: _____

Quality of product: _____

Any missing items: _____

Customer service notes: _____

_____

If the kit was a gift, who was it from? _____

Date gift received: _____   Occasion: _____

Date started: _____   Date completed: _____

Estimated total hours to complete: _____

Difficulty level: Beginner ▽   Intermediate ▽   Advanced ▽

What I did with the finished piece:

Kept it ▽   Gifted it ▽   Sold it ▽   Other _____

If gifted or sold, person received: _____

If sold, what was the price? _____

Framed: Yes ▽   No ▽

My overall rating of this project: ▽ ▽ ▽ ▽ ▽

Diamond Painting Photo

Additional notes: _____

_____

_____

_____

_____

_____

_____

_____

_____

_____

_____

Design/kit name: _____

If custom, describe: _____

Dimensions: _____

Drill type: Square ▽   Round ▽   Special ▽

Drill total: _____   Coverage: Full ▽   Partial ▽

Number of different drill colors: _____

Website purchased from: _____

Seller/store name: _____

Price: _____   On Sale: Yes ▽   No ▽

Shipping cost: _____   Estimated arrival date: _____

Date purchased: _____

Date arrived: _____

Quality of product: _____

Any missing items: _____

Customer service notes: _____

_____

If the kit was a gift, who was it from? _____

Date gift received: _____   Occasion: _____

Date started: _____   Date completed: _____

Estimated total hours to complete: _____

Difficulty level: Beginner ▽   Intermediate ▽   Advanced ▽

What I did with the finished piece:

Kept it ▽   Gifted it ▽   Sold it ▽   Other _____

If gifted or sold, person received: _____

If sold, what was the price? _____

Framed: Yes ▽   No ▽

My overall rating of this project: ▽ ▽ ▽ ▽ ▽

Diamond Painting Photo

Additional notes: _____

_____
_____
_____
_____
_____
_____
_____
_____
_____
_____
_____

Design/kit name: _____

If custom, describe: _____

Dimensions: _____

Drill type: Square ▽   Round ▽   Special ▽

Drill total: _____   Coverage: Full ▽   Partial ▽

Number of different drill colors: _____

Website purchased from: _____

Seller/store name: _____

Price: _____   On Sale: Yes ▽   No ▽

Shipping cost: _____   Estimated arrival date: _____

Date purchased: _____

Date arrived: _____

Quality of product: _____

Any missing items: _____

Customer service notes: _____

_____

If the kit was a gift, who was it from? _____

Date gift received: _____   Occasion: _____

Date started: _____   Date completed: _____

Estimated total hours to complete: _____

Difficulty level: Beginner ▽   Intermediate ▽   Advanced ▽

What I did with the finished piece:

Kept it ▽   Gifted it ▽   Sold it ▽   Other _____

If gifted or sold, person received: _____

If sold, what was the price? _____

Framed: Yes ▽   No ▽

My overall rating of this project: ▽ ▽ ▽ ▽ ▽

Diamond Painting Photo

Additional notes: _____

_____
_____
_____
_____
_____
_____
_____
_____
_____
_____

Design/kit name: _____

If custom, describe: _____

Dimensions: _____

Drill type: Square ▽   Round ▽   Special ▽

Drill total: _____   Coverage: Full ▽   Partial ▽

Number of different drill colors: _____

Website purchased from: _____

Seller/store name: _____

Price: _____   On Sale: Yes ▽   No ▽

Shipping cost: _____   Estimated arrival date: _____

Date purchased: _____

Date arrived: _____

Quality of product: _____

Any missing items: _____

Customer service notes: _____

_____

If the kit was a gift, who was it from? _____

Date gift received: _____   Occasion: _____

Date started: _____   Date completed: _____

Estimated total hours to complete: _____

Difficulty level: Beginner ▽   Intermediate ▽   Advanced ▽

What I did with the finished piece:

Kept it ▽   Gifted it ▽   Sold it ▽   Other _____

If gifted or sold, person received: _____

If sold, what was the price? _____

Framed: Yes ▽   No ▽

My overall rating of this project: ▽ ▽ ▽ ▽ ▽

Diamond Painting Photo

Additional notes: _____

_____

_____

_____

_____

_____

_____

_____

_____

_____

_____

Design/kit name: _____

If custom, describe: _____

Dimensions: _____

Drill type: Square ▽   Round ▽   Special ▽

Drill total: _____   Coverage: Full ▽   Partial ▽

Number of different drill colors: _____

Website purchased from: _____

Seller/store name: _____

Price: _____   On Sale: Yes ▽   No ▽

Shipping cost: _____   Estimated arrival date: _____

Date purchased: _____

Date arrived: _____

Quality of product: _____

Any missing items: _____

Customer service notes: _____

_____

If the kit was a gift, who was it from? _____

Date gift received: _____   Occasion: _____

Date started: _____   Date completed: _____

Estimated total hours to complete: _____

Difficulty level: Beginner ▽   Intermediate ▽   Advanced ▽

What I did with the finished piece:

Kept it ▽   Gifted it ▽   Sold it ▽   Other _____

If gifted or sold, person received: _____

If sold, what was the price? _____

Framed: Yes ▽   No ▽

My overall rating of this project: ▽ ▽ ▽ ▽ ▽

Diamond Painting Photo

Additional notes: _____

_____

_____

_____

_____

_____

_____

_____

_____

_____

_____

Design/kit name: _____

If custom, describe: _____

Dimensions: _____

Drill type: Square ▽   Round ▽   Special ▽

Drill total: _____   Coverage: Full ▽   Partial ▽

Number of different drill colors: _____

Website purchased from: _____

Seller/store name: _____

Price: _____   On Sale: Yes ▽   No ▽

Shipping cost: _____   Estimated arrival date: _____

Date purchased: _____

Date arrived: _____

Quality of product: _____

Any missing items: _____

Customer service notes: _____

_____

If the kit was a gift, who was it from? _____

Date gift received: _____   Occasion: _____

Date started: _____   Date completed: _____

Estimated total hours to complete: _____

Difficulty level: Beginner ▽   Intermediate ▽   Advanced ▽

What I did with the finished piece:

Kept it ▽   Gifted it ▽   Sold it ▽   Other _____

If gifted or sold, person received: _____

If sold, what was the price? _____

Framed: Yes ▽   No ▽

My overall rating of this project: ▽ ▽ ▽ ▽ ▽

Diamond Painting Photo

Additional notes: _____

_____

_____

_____

_____

_____

_____

_____

_____

_____

_____

Design/kit name: _____

If custom, describe: _____

Dimensions: _____

Drill type: Square ▽   Round ▽   Special ▽

Drill total: _____   Coverage: Full ▽   Partial ▽

Number of different drill colors: _____

Website purchased from: _____

Seller/store name: _____

Price: _____   On Sale: Yes ▽   No ▽

Shipping cost: _____   Estimated arrival date: _____

Date purchased: _____

Date arrived: _____

Quality of product: _____

Any missing items: _____

Customer service notes: _____

_____

If the kit was a gift, who was it from? _____

Date gift received: _____   Occasion: _____

Date started: _____   Date completed: _____

Estimated total hours to complete: _____

Difficulty level: Beginner ▽   Intermediate ▽   Advanced ▽

What I did with the finished piece:

Kept it ▽   Gifted it ▽   Sold it ▽   Other _____

If gifted or sold, person received: _____

If sold, what was the price? _____

Framed: Yes ▽   No ▽

My overall rating of this project: ▽ ▽ ▽ ▽ ▽

Diamond Painting Photo

Additional notes: _____

_____
_____
_____
_____
_____
_____
_____
_____
_____
_____
_____

Design/kit name: _____

If custom, describe: _____

Dimensions: _____

Drill type: Square ▽   Round ▽   Special ▽

Drill total: _____   Coverage: Full ▽   Partial ▽

Number of different drill colors: _____

Website purchased from: _____

Seller/store name: _____

Price: _____   On Sale: Yes ▽   No ▽

Shipping cost: _____   Estimated arrival date: _____

Date purchased: _____

Date arrived: _____

Quality of product: _____

Any missing items: _____

Customer service notes: _____

_____

If the kit was a gift, who was it from? _____

Date gift received: _____   Occasion: _____

Date started: _____   Date completed: _____

Estimated total hours to complete: _____

Difficulty level: Beginner ▽   Intermediate ▽   Advanced ▽

What I did with the finished piece:

Kept it ▽   Gifted it ▽   Sold it ▽   Other _____

If gifted or sold, person received: _____

If sold, what was the price? _____

Framed: Yes ▽   No ▽

My overall rating of this project: ▽ ▽ ▽ ▽ ▽

Diamond Painting Photo

Additional notes: _____

_____

_____

_____

_____

_____

_____

_____

_____

_____

_____

_____

Design/kit name: _____

If custom, describe: _____

Dimensions: _____

Drill type: Square ▽   Round ▽   Special ▽

Drill total: _____   Coverage: Full ▽   Partial ▽

Number of different drill colors: _____

Website purchased from: _____

Seller/store name: _____

Price: _____   On Sale: Yes ▽   No ▽

Shipping cost: _____   Estimated arrival date: _____

Date purchased: _____

Date arrived: _____

Quality of product: _____

Any missing items: _____

Customer service notes: _____

_____

If the kit was a gift, who was it from? _____

Date gift received: _____   Occasion: _____

Date started: _____   Date completed: _____

Estimated total hours to complete: _____

Difficulty level: Beginner ▽   Intermediate ▽   Advanced ▽

What I did with the finished piece:

Kept it ▽   Gifted it ▽   Sold it ▽   Other _____

If gifted or sold, person received: _____

If sold, what was the price? _____

Framed: Yes ▽   No ▽

My overall rating of this project: ▽ ▽ ▽ ▽ ▽

Diamond Painting Photo

Additional notes: _____

_____
_____
_____
_____
_____
_____
_____
_____
_____
_____

Design/kit name: _____

If custom, describe: _____

Dimensions: _____

Drill type: Square ▽   Round ▽   Special ▽

Drill total: _____   Coverage: Full ▽   Partial ▽

Number of different drill colors: _____

Website purchased from: _____

Seller/store name: _____

Price: _____   On Sale: Yes ▽   No ▽

Shipping cost: _____   Estimated arrival date: _____

Date purchased: _____

Date arrived: _____

Quality of product: _____

Any missing items: _____

Customer service notes: _____

_____

If the kit was a gift, who was it from? _____

Date gift received: _____   Occasion: _____

Date started: _____   Date completed: _____

Estimated total hours to complete: _____

Difficulty level: Beginner ▽   Intermediate ▽   Advanced ▽

What I did with the finished piece:

Kept it ▽   Gifted it ▽   Sold it ▽   Other _____

If gifted or sold, person received: _____

If sold, what was the price? _____

Framed: Yes ▽   No ▽

My overall rating of this project: ▽ ▽ ▽ ▽ ▽

Diamond Painting Photo

Additional notes: _____

_____

_____

_____

_____

_____

_____

_____

_____

_____

_____

Design/kit name: _____

If custom, describe: _____

Dimensions: _____

Drill type: Square ▽   Round ▽   Special ▽

Drill total: _____   Coverage: Full ▽   Partial ▽

Number of different drill colors: _____

Website purchased from: _____

Seller/store name: _____

Price: _____   On Sale: Yes ▽   No ▽

Shipping cost: _____   Estimated arrival date: _____

Date purchased: _____

Date arrived: _____

Quality of product: _____

Any missing items: _____

Customer service notes: _____

_____

If the kit was a gift, who was it from? _____

Date gift received: _____   Occasion: _____

Date started: _____   Date completed: _____

Estimated total hours to complete: _____

Difficulty level: Beginner ▽   Intermediate ▽   Advanced ▽

What I did with the finished piece:

Kept it ▽   Gifted it ▽   Sold it ▽   Other _____

If gifted or sold, person received: _____

If sold, what was the price? _____

Framed: Yes ▽   No ▽

My overall rating of this project: ▽ ▽ ▽ ▽ ▽

Diamond Painting Photo

Additional notes: _____

_____

_____

_____

_____

_____

_____

_____

_____

_____

_____

Design/kit name: _____

If custom, describe: _____

Dimensions: _____

Drill type:　Square ▽　　Round ▽　　Special ▽

Drill total: _____　Coverage:　Full ▽　Partial ▽

Number of different drill colors: _____

Website purchased from: _____

Seller/store name: _____

Price: _____　On Sale:　Yes ▽　　No ▽

Shipping cost: _____　Estimated arrival date: _____

Date purchased: _____

Date arrived: _____

Quality of product: _____

Any missing items: _____

Customer service notes: _____

_____

If the kit was a gift, who was it from? _____

Date gift received: _____　Occasion: _____

Date started: _____　Date completed: _____

Estimated total hours to complete: _____

Difficulty level:　Beginner ▽　Intermediate ▽　Advanced ▽

What I did with the finished piece:

Kept it ▽　Gifted it ▽　Sold it ▽　Other _____

If gifted or sold, person received: _____

If sold, what was the price? _____

Framed:　Yes ▽　　No ▽

My overall rating of this project:　▽ ▽ ▽ ▽ ▽

Diamond Painting Photo

Additional notes: _____

_____
_____
_____
_____
_____
_____
_____
_____
_____
_____
_____

Design/kit name: _____

If custom, describe: _____

Dimensions: _____

Drill type:　Square ▽　　Round ▽　　Special ▽

Drill total: _____　Coverage:　Full ▽　Partial ▽

Number of different drill colors: _____

Website purchased from: _____

Seller/store name: _____

Price: _____　On Sale:　Yes ▽　　No ▽

Shipping cost: _____　Estimated arrival date: _____

Date purchased: _____

Date arrived: _____

Quality of product: _____

Any missing items: _____

Customer service notes: _____

_____

If the kit was a gift, who was it from? _____

Date gift received: _____　Occasion: _____

Date started: _____　Date completed: _____

Estimated total hours to complete: _____

Difficulty level:　Beginner ▽　Intermediate ▽　Advanced ▽

What I did with the finished piece:

Kept it ▽　　Gifted it ▽　　Sold it ▽　Other _____

If gifted or sold, person received: _____

If sold, what was the price? _____

Framed:　Yes ▽　　No ▽

My overall rating of this project:　▽ ▽ ▽ ▽ ▽

Diamond Painting Photo

Additional notes: _____

_____

_____

_____

_____

_____

_____

_____

_____

_____

Design/kit name: _____

If custom, describe: _____

Dimensions: _____

Drill type: Square ▽   Round ▽   Special ▽

Drill total: _____   Coverage: Full ▽   Partial ▽

Number of different drill colors: _____

Website purchased from: _____

Seller/store name: _____

Price: _____   On Sale: Yes ▽   No ▽

Shipping cost: _____   Estimated arrival date: _____

Date purchased: _____

Date arrived: _____

Quality of product: _____

Any missing items: _____

Customer service notes: _____

_____

If the kit was a gift, who was it from? _____

Date gift received: _____   Occasion: _____

Date started: _____   Date completed: _____

Estimated total hours to complete: _____

Difficulty level: Beginner ▽   Intermediate ▽   Advanced ▽

What I did with the finished piece:

Kept it ▽   Gifted it ▽   Sold it ▽   Other _____

If gifted or sold, person received: _____

If sold, what was the price? _____

Framed: Yes ▽   No ▽

My overall rating of this project: ▽ ▽ ▽ ▽ ▽

Diamond Painting Photo

Additional notes: _____

_____

_____

_____

_____

_____

_____

_____

_____

_____

_____

Design/kit name: _____

If custom, describe: _____

Dimensions: _____

Drill type: Square ▽   Round ▽   Special ▽

Drill total: _____   Coverage: Full ▽   Partial ▽

Number of different drill colors: _____

Website purchased from: _____

Seller/store name: _____

Price: _____   On Sale: Yes ▽   No ▽

Shipping cost: _____   Estimated arrival date: _____

Date purchased: _____

Date arrived: _____

Quality of product: _____

Any missing items: _____

Customer service notes: _____

_____

If the kit was a gift, who was it from? _____

Date gift received: _____   Occasion: _____

Date started: _____   Date completed: _____

Estimated total hours to complete: _____

Difficulty level: Beginner ▽   Intermediate ▽   Advanced ▽

What I did with the finished piece:

Kept it ▽   Gifted it ▽   Sold it ▽   Other _____

If gifted or sold, person received: _____

If sold, what was the price? _____

Framed: Yes ▽   No ▽

My overall rating of this project: ▽ ▽ ▽ ▽ ▽

Diamond Painting Photo

Additional notes: _____

_____

_____

_____

_____

_____

_____

_____

_____

_____

_____

Design/kit name: _____

If custom, describe: _____

Dimensions: _____

Drill type: Square ▽   Round ▽   Special ▽

Drill total: _____   Coverage: Full ▽   Partial ▽

Number of different drill colors: _____

Website purchased from: _____

Seller/store name: _____

Price: _____   On Sale: Yes ▽   No ▽

Shipping cost: _____   Estimated arrival date: _____

Date purchased: _____

Date arrived: _____

Quality of product: _____

Any missing items: _____

Customer service notes: _____

_____

If the kit was a gift, who was it from? _____

Date gift received: _____   Occasion: _____

Date started: _____   Date completed: _____

Estimated total hours to complete: _____

Difficulty level: Beginner ▽   Intermediate ▽   Advanced ▽

What I did with the finished piece:

Kept it ▽   Gifted it ▽   Sold it ▽   Other _____

If gifted or sold, person received: _____

If sold, what was the price? _____

Framed: Yes ▽   No ▽

My overall rating of this project: ▽ ▽ ▽ ▽ ▽

Diamond Painting Photo

Additional notes: _____

_____
_____
_____
_____
_____
_____
_____
_____
_____
_____
_____

Design/kit name: _____

If custom, describe: _____

Dimensions: _____

Drill type: Square ▽   Round ▽   Special ▽

Drill total: _____   Coverage: Full ▽   Partial ▽

Number of different drill colors: _____

Website purchased from: _____

Seller/store name: _____

Price: _____   On Sale: Yes ▽   No ▽

Shipping cost: _____   Estimated arrival date: _____

Date purchased: _____

Date arrived: _____

Quality of product: _____

Any missing items: _____

Customer service notes: _____

_____

If the kit was a gift, who was it from? _____

Date gift received: _____   Occasion: _____

Date started: _____   Date completed: _____

Estimated total hours to complete: _____

Difficulty level: Beginner ▽   Intermediate ▽   Advanced ▽

What I did with the finished piece:

Kept it ▽   Gifted it ▽   Sold it ▽   Other _____

If gifted or sold, person received: _____

If sold, what was the price? _____

Framed: Yes ▽   No ▽

My overall rating of this project: ▽ ▽ ▽ ▽ ▽

Diamond Painting Photo

Additional notes: _____

_____

_____

_____

_____

_____

_____

_____

_____

_____

_____

Design/kit name: _____

If custom, describe: _____

Dimensions: _____

Drill type: Square ▽   Round ▽   Special ▽

Drill total: _____   Coverage: Full ▽   Partial ▽

Number of different drill colors: _____

Website purchased from: _____

Seller/store name: _____

Price: _____   On Sale: Yes ▽   No ▽

Shipping cost: _____   Estimated arrival date: _____

Date purchased: _____

Date arrived: _____

Quality of product: _____

Any missing items: _____

Customer service notes: _____

_____

If the kit was a gift, who was it from? _____

Date gift received: _____   Occasion: _____

Date started: _____   Date completed: _____

Estimated total hours to complete: _____

Difficulty level: Beginner ▽   Intermediate ▽   Advanced ▽

What I did with the finished piece:

Kept it ▽   Gifted it ▽   Sold it ▽   Other _____

If gifted or sold, person received: _____

If sold, what was the price? _____

Framed: Yes ▽   No ▽

My overall rating of this project: ▽ ▽ ▽ ▽ ▽

Diamond Painting Photo

Additional notes: _____

_____
_____
_____
_____
_____
_____
_____
_____
_____

Design/kit name: _____

If custom, describe: _____

Dimensions: _____

Drill type: Square ▽   Round ▽   Special ▽

Drill total: _____   Coverage: Full ▽   Partial ▽

Number of different drill colors: _____

Website purchased from: _____

Seller/store name: _____

Price: _____   On Sale: Yes ▽   No ▽

Shipping cost: _____   Estimated arrival date: _____

Date purchased: _____

Date arrived: _____

Quality of product: _____

Any missing items: _____

Customer service notes: _____

_____

If the kit was a gift, who was it from? _____

Date gift received: _____   Occasion: _____

Date started: _____   Date completed: _____

Estimated total hours to complete: _____

Difficulty level: Beginner ▽   Intermediate ▽   Advanced ▽

What I did with the finished piece:

Kept it ▽   Gifted it ▽   Sold it ▽   Other _____

If gifted or sold, person received: _____

If sold, what was the price? _____

Framed: Yes ▽   No ▽

My overall rating of this project: ▽ ▽ ▽ ▽ ▽

Diamond Painting Photo

Additional notes: _____

_____

_____

_____

_____

_____

_____

_____

_____

_____

_____

Design/kit name: _____

If custom, describe: _____

Dimensions: _____

Drill type: Square ▽   Round ▽   Special ▽

Drill total: _____   Coverage: Full ▽   Partial ▽

Number of different drill colors: _____

Website purchased from: _____

Seller/store name: _____

Price: _____   On Sale: Yes ▽   No ▽

Shipping cost: _____   Estimated arrival date: _____

Date purchased: _____

Date arrived: _____

Quality of product: _____

Any missing items: _____

Customer service notes: _____

_____

If the kit was a gift, who was it from? _____

Date gift received: _____   Occasion: _____

Date started: _____   Date completed: _____

Estimated total hours to complete: _____

Difficulty level: Beginner ▽   Intermediate ▽   Advanced ▽

What I did with the finished piece:

Kept it ▽   Gifted it ▽   Sold it ▽   Other _____

If gifted or sold, person received: _____

If sold, what was the price? _____

Framed: Yes ▽   No ▽

My overall rating of this project: ▽ ▽ ▽ ▽ ▽

Diamond Painting Photo

Additional notes: _____

_____

_____

_____

_____

_____

_____

_____

_____

_____

_____

_____

Design/kit name: _____

If custom, describe: _____

Dimensions: _____

Drill type: Square ▽   Round ▽   Special ▽

Drill total: _____   Coverage: Full ▽   Partial ▽

Number of different drill colors: _____

Website purchased from: _____

Seller/store name: _____

Price: _____   On Sale: Yes ▽   No ▽

Shipping cost: _____   Estimated arrival date: _____

Date purchased: _____

Date arrived: _____

Quality of product: _____

Any missing items: _____

Customer service notes: _____

_____

If the kit was a gift, who was it from? _____

Date gift received: _____   Occasion: _____

Date started: _____   Date completed: _____

Estimated total hours to complete: _____

Difficulty level: Beginner ▽   Intermediate ▽   Advanced ▽

What I did with the finished piece:

Kept it ▽   Gifted it ▽   Sold it ▽   Other _____

If gifted or sold, person received: _____

If sold, what was the price? _____

Framed: Yes ▽   No ▽

My overall rating of this project: ▽ ▽ ▽ ▽ ▽

Diamond Painting Photo

Additional notes: _____

_____
_____
_____
_____
_____
_____
_____
_____
_____
_____
_____

Design/kit name: _____

If custom, describe: _____

Dimensions: _____

Drill type: Square ▽   Round ▽   Special ▽

Drill total: _____   Coverage: Full ▽   Partial ▽

Number of different drill colors: _____

Website purchased from: _____

Seller/store name: _____

Price: _____   On Sale: Yes ▽   No ▽

Shipping cost: _____   Estimated arrival date: _____

Date purchased: _____

Date arrived: _____

Quality of product: _____

Any missing items: _____

Customer service notes: _____

_____

If the kit was a gift, who was it from? _____

Date gift received: _____   Occasion: _____

Date started: _____   Date completed: _____

Estimated total hours to complete: _____

Difficulty level: Beginner ▽   Intermediate ▽   Advanced ▽

What I did with the finished piece:

Kept it ▽   Gifted it ▽   Sold it ▽   Other _____

If gifted or sold, person received: _____

If sold, what was the price? _____

Framed: Yes ▽   No ▽

My overall rating of this project: ▽ ▽ ▽ ▽ ▽

Diamond Painting Photo

Additional notes: _____

_____

_____

_____

_____

_____

_____

_____

_____

_____

_____

_____

Design/kit name: _____

If custom, describe: _____

Dimensions: _____

Drill type:　Square ▽　　　Round ▽　　　Special ▽

Drill total: _____　Coverage:　Full ▽　Partial ▽

Number of different drill colors: _____

Website purchased from: _____

Seller/store name: _____

Price: _____　On Sale:　Yes ▽　　No ▽

Shipping cost: _____　Estimated arrival date: _____

Date purchased: _____

Date arrived: _____

Quality of product: _____

Any missing items: _____

Customer service notes: _____

_____

If the kit was a gift, who was it from? _____

Date gift received: _____　Occasion: _____

Date started: _____　Date completed: _____

Estimated total hours to complete: _____

Difficulty level:　Beginner ▽　Intermediate ▽　Advanced ▽

What I did with the finished piece:

Kept it ▽　　Gifted it ▽　　Sold it ▽　　Other _____

If gifted or sold, person received: _____

If sold, what was the price? _____

Framed:　Yes ▽　　No ▽

My overall rating of this project:　▽ ▽ ▽ ▽ ▽

Diamond Painting Photo

Additional notes: _____

_____
_____
_____
_____
_____
_____
_____
_____
_____
_____

Design/kit name: _____

If custom, describe: _____

Dimensions: _____

Drill type:　Square ▽　　Round ▽　　Special ▽

Drill total: _____　Coverage:　Full ▽　Partial ▽

Number of different drill colors: _____

Website purchased from: _____

Seller/store name: _____

Price: _____　On Sale:　Yes ▽　　No ▽

Shipping cost: _____　Estimated arrival date: _____

Date purchased: _____

Date arrived: _____

Quality of product: _____

Any missing items: _____

Customer service notes: _____

_____

If the kit was a gift, who was it from? _____

Date gift received: _____　Occasion: _____

Date started: _____　Date completed: _____

Estimated total hours to complete: _____

Difficulty level:　Beginner ▽　　Intermediate ▽　　Advanced ▽

What I did with the finished piece:

Kept it ▽　　Gifted it ▽　　Sold it ▽　　Other _____

If gifted or sold, person received: _____

If sold, what was the price? _____

Framed:　Yes ▽　　No ▽

My overall rating of this project:　▽ ▽ ▽ ▽ ▽

Diamond Painting Photo

Additional notes: _____

_____

_____

_____

_____

_____

_____

_____

_____

_____

_____

Design/kit name: _____

If custom, describe: _____

Dimensions: _____

Drill type: Square ▽   Round ▽   Special ▽

Drill total: _____   Coverage: Full ▽   Partial ▽

Number of different drill colors: _____

Website purchased from: _____

Seller/store name: _____

Price: _____   On Sale: Yes ▽   No ▽

Shipping cost: _____   Estimated arrival date: _____

Date purchased: _____

Date arrived: _____

Quality of product: _____

Any missing items: _____

Customer service notes: _____

_____

If the kit was a gift, who was it from? _____

Date gift received: _____   Occasion: _____

Date started: _____   Date completed: _____

Estimated total hours to complete: _____

Difficulty level: Beginner ▽   Intermediate ▽   Advanced ▽

What I did with the finished piece:

Kept it ▽   Gifted it ▽   Sold it ▽   Other _____

If gifted or sold, person received: _____

If sold, what was the price? _____

Framed: Yes ▽   No ▽

My overall rating of this project: ▽ ▽ ▽ ▽ ▽

Diamond Painting Photo

Additional notes: _____

_____
_____
_____
_____
_____
_____
_____
_____
_____
_____

Design/kit name: _____

If custom, describe: _____

Dimensions: _____

Drill type: Square ▽   Round ▽   Special ▽

Drill total: _____   Coverage: Full ▽   Partial ▽

Number of different drill colors: _____

Website purchased from: _____

Seller/store name: _____

Price: _____   On Sale: Yes ▽   No ▽

Shipping cost: _____   Estimated arrival date: _____

Date purchased: _____

Date arrived: _____

Quality of product: _____

Any missing items: _____

Customer service notes: _____

_____

If the kit was a gift, who was it from? _____

Date gift received: _____   Occasion: _____

Date started: _____   Date completed: _____

Estimated total hours to complete: _____

Difficulty level: Beginner ▽   Intermediate ▽   Advanced ▽

What I did with the finished piece:

Kept it ▽   Gifted it ▽   Sold it ▽   Other _____

If gifted or sold, person received: _____

If sold, what was the price? _____

Framed: Yes ▽   No ▽

My overall rating of this project: ▽ ▽ ▽ ▽ ▽

Diamond Painting Photo

Additional notes: _____

_____

_____

_____

_____

_____

_____

_____

_____

_____

_____

Design/kit name: _____

If custom, describe: _____

Dimensions: _____

Drill type: Square $\triangledown$ Round $\triangledown$ Special $\triangledown$

Drill total: _____   Coverage: Full $\triangledown$ Partial $\triangledown$

Number of different drill colors: _____

Website purchased from: _____

Seller/store name: _____

Price: _____   On Sale: Yes $\triangledown$ No $\triangledown$

Shipping cost: _____   Estimated arrival date: _____

Date purchased: _____

Date arrived: _____

Quality of product: _____

Any missing items: _____

Customer service notes: _____

_____

If the kit was a gift, who was it from? _____

Date gift received: _____   Occasion: _____

Date started: _____   Date completed: _____

Estimated total hours to complete: _____

Difficulty level: Beginner $\triangledown$ Intermediate $\triangledown$ Advanced $\triangledown$

What I did with the finished piece:

Kept it $\triangledown$ Gifted it $\triangledown$ Sold it $\triangledown$ Other _____

If gifted or sold, person received: _____

If sold, what was the price? _____

Framed: Yes $\triangledown$ No $\triangledown$

My overall rating of this project: $\triangledown$ $\triangledown$ $\triangledown$ $\triangledown$ $\triangledown$

Diamond Painting Photo

Additional notes: _____

_____

_____

_____

_____

_____

_____

_____

_____

_____

_____

Design/kit name: _____

If custom, describe: _____

Dimensions: _____

Drill type: Square ▽   Round ▽   Special ▽

Drill total: _____   Coverage: Full ▽   Partial ▽

Number of different drill colors: _____

Website purchased from: _____

Seller/store name: _____

Price: _____   On Sale: Yes ▽   No ▽

Shipping cost: _____   Estimated arrival date: _____

Date purchased: _____

Date arrived: _____

Quality of product: _____

Any missing items: _____

Customer service notes: _____

_____

If the kit was a gift, who was it from? _____

Date gift received: _____   Occasion: _____

Date started: _____   Date completed: _____

Estimated total hours to complete: _____

Difficulty level: Beginner ▽   Intermediate ▽   Advanced ▽

What I did with the finished piece:

Kept it ▽   Gifted it ▽   Sold it ▽   Other _____

If gifted or sold, person received: _____

If sold, what was the price? _____

Framed: Yes ▽   No ▽

My overall rating of this project: ▽ ▽ ▽ ▽ ▽

Diamond Painting Photo

Additional notes: _____

_____
_____
_____
_____
_____
_____
_____
_____
_____
_____
_____

Design/kit name: _____

If custom, describe: _____

Dimensions: _____

Drill type: Square ▽   Round ▽   Special ▽

Drill total: _____   Coverage: Full ▽   Partial ▽

Number of different drill colors: _____

Website purchased from: _____

Seller/store name: _____

Price: _____   On Sale: Yes ▽   No ▽

Shipping cost: _____   Estimated arrival date: _____

Date purchased: _____

Date arrived: _____

Quality of product: _____

Any missing items: _____

Customer service notes: _____

_____

If the kit was a gift, who was it from? _____

Date gift received: _____   Occasion: _____

Date started: _____   Date completed: _____

Estimated total hours to complete: _____

Difficulty level: Beginner ▽   Intermediate ▽   Advanced ▽

What I did with the finished piece:

Kept it ▽   Gifted it ▽   Sold it ▽   Other _____

If gifted or sold, person received: _____

If sold, what was the price? _____

Framed: Yes ▽   No ▽

My overall rating of this project: ▽ ▽ ▽ ▽ ▽

Diamond Painting Photo

Additional notes: _____

_____

_____

_____

_____

_____

_____

_____

_____

_____

_____

Design/kit name: _____

If custom, describe: _____

Dimensions: _____

Drill type: Square ▽   Round ▽   Special ▽

Drill total: _____   Coverage: Full ▽   Partial ▽

Number of different drill colors: _____

Website purchased from: _____

Seller/store name: _____

Price: _____   On Sale: Yes ▽   No ▽

Shipping cost: _____   Estimated arrival date: _____

Date purchased: _____

Date arrived: _____

Quality of product: _____

Any missing items: _____

Customer service notes: _____

_____

If the kit was a gift, who was it from? _____

Date gift received: _____   Occasion: _____

Date started: _____   Date completed: _____

Estimated total hours to complete: _____

Difficulty level: Beginner ▽   Intermediate ▽   Advanced ▽

What I did with the finished piece:

Kept it ▽   Gifted it ▽   Sold it ▽   Other _____

If gifted or sold, person received: _____

If sold, what was the price? _____

Framed: Yes ▽   No ▽

My overall rating of this project: ▽ ▽ ▽ ▽ ▽

Diamond Painting Photo

Additional notes: _____

_____
_____
_____
_____
_____
_____
_____
_____
_____
_____
_____

Design/kit name: _____

If custom, describe: _____

Dimensions: _____

Drill type: Square ▽   Round ▽   Special ▽

Drill total: _____   Coverage: Full ▽   Partial ▽

Number of different drill colors: _____

Website purchased from: _____

Seller/store name: _____

Price: _____   On Sale: Yes ▽   No ▽

Shipping cost: _____   Estimated arrival date: _____

Date purchased: _____

Date arrived: _____

Quality of product: _____

Any missing items: _____

Customer service notes: _____

_____

If the kit was a gift, who was it from? _____

Date gift received: _____   Occasion: _____

Date started: _____   Date completed: _____

Estimated total hours to complete: _____

Difficulty level: Beginner ▽   Intermediate ▽   Advanced ▽

What I did with the finished piece:

Kept it ▽   Gifted it ▽   Sold it ▽   Other _____

If gifted or sold, person received: _____

If sold, what was the price? _____

Framed: Yes ▽   No ▽

My overall rating of this project: ▽ ▽ ▽ ▽ ▽

Diamond Painting Photo

Additional notes: _____

_____

_____

_____

_____

_____

_____

_____

_____

_____

_____

Design/kit name: _____

If custom, describe: _____

Dimensions: _____

Drill type: Square ▽   Round ▽   Special ▽

Drill total: _____   Coverage: Full ▽   Partial ▽

Number of different drill colors: _____

Website purchased from: _____

Seller/store name: _____

Price: _____   On Sale: Yes ▽   No ▽

Shipping cost: _____   Estimated arrival date: _____

Date purchased: _____

Date arrived: _____

Quality of product: _____

Any missing items: _____

Customer service notes: _____

_____

If the kit was a gift, who was it from? _____

Date gift received: _____   Occasion: _____

Date started: _____   Date completed: _____

Estimated total hours to complete: _____

Difficulty level: Beginner ▽   Intermediate ▽   Advanced ▽

What I did with the finished piece:

Kept it ▽   Gifted it ▽   Sold it ▽   Other _____

If gifted or sold, person received: _____

If sold, what was the price? _____

Framed: Yes ▽   No ▽

My overall rating of this project: ▽ ▽ ▽ ▽ ▽

Diamond Painting Photo

Additional notes: _____

_____
_____
_____
_____
_____
_____
_____
_____
_____
_____
_____

Design/kit name: _____

If custom, describe: _____

Dimensions: _____

Drill type:　Square ▽　　Round ▽　　Special ▽

Drill total: _____　Coverage:　Full ▽　Partial ▽

Number of different drill colors: _____

Website purchased from: _____

Seller/store name: _____

Price: _____　On Sale:　Yes ▽　　No ▽

Shipping cost: _____　Estimated arrival date: _____

Date purchased: _____

Date arrived: _____

Quality of product: _____

Any missing items: _____

Customer service notes: _____

_____

If the kit was a gift, who was it from? _____

Date gift received: _____　Occasion: _____

Date started: _____　Date completed: _____

Estimated total hours to complete: _____

Difficulty level:　Beginner ▽　Intermediate ▽　Advanced ▽

What I did with the finished piece:

Kept it ▽　　Gifted it ▽　　Sold it ▽　　Other _____

If gifted or sold, person received: _____

If sold, what was the price? _____

Framed:　Yes ▽　　No ▽

My overall rating of this project:　▽ ▽ ▽ ▽ ▽

Diamond Painting Summary

for projects tracked in this book from

Date: _____ *to* **Date:** _____

Total Kits Bought: _____

Total Custom Kits Bought: _____

Total Money Spent: _____

Highest Priced Kit: _____   Lowest Priced Kit: _____

Largest Size: _____   Smallest Size: _____

Longest Time to Complete a Painting: _____

Shortest Time to Complete a Painting: _____

Total Paintings Kept: _____

Total Paintings Gifted: _____

Total Paintings Sold: _____

Total Partial Drill Paintings: _____

Total Full Drill Paintings: _____

Top 5 Favorite Paintings:

Design: _____   Page: _____

Design: _____   Page: _____

Design: _____   Page: _____

Design: _____   Page: _____

Design: _____   Page: _____

Least Favorite Painting: _____   Page: _____

Top 5 Preferred Purchase Sites/Sellers:

_____

_____

_____

_____

_____

Favorite Diamond Painting Social Media Groups

_____

_____

_____

_____

_____

_____

_____

_____

Favorite Diamond Painting YouTube Channels

_____

_____

_____

_____

_____

_____

Favorite Diamond Painting Blogs

_____

_____

_____

_____

_____

_____

Diamond Painting Raffles I've Won

Kit Name	Date	Cost	From

Diamond Painting Tips & Tricks

_____

_____

_____

_____

_____

_____

_____

_____

_____

_____

_____

_____

_____

_____

_____

Diamond Painting Friends

Name: _____

Email: _____

Phone: _____

Where we met: _____

Name: _____

Email: _____

Phone: _____

Where we met: _____

Name: _____

Email: _____

Phone: _____

Where we met: _____

Name: _____

Email: _____

Phone: _____

Where we met: _____

Name: _____

Email: _____

Phone: _____

Where we met: _____

Name: _____

Email: _____

Phone: _____

Where we met: _____

Accessories or Tools I've Purchased

_____

_____

_____

_____

_____

_____

_____

_____

_____

Accessories or Tools on My Wish List

_____

_____

_____

_____

_____

_____

_____

_____

_____

_____

_____

_____

_____

Additional Notes

Quick Reference Index

Pages	Design
1-2	
3-4	
5-6	
7-8	
9-10	
11-12	
13-14	
15-16	
17-18	
19-20	
21-22	
23-24	
25-26	
27-28	
29-30	
31-32	
33-34	
35-36	
37-38	
39-40	
41-42	
43-44	
45-46	
47-48	
49-50	
51-52	
53-54	
55-56	
57-58	
59-60	

Quick Reference Index

Pages	Design
61-62	
63-64	
65-66	
67-68	
69-70	
71-72	
73-74	
75-76	
77-78	
79-80	
81-82	
83-84	
85-86	
87-88	
89-90	
91-92	
93-94	
95-96	
97-98	
99-100	
101-102	
103-104	
105-106	
107-108	
109-110	
111-112	
113-114	
115-116	
117-118	
119-120	

Time to grab another
Diamond Painting Log Book

Made in United States
Orlando, FL
14 March 2022

15784892R00075